YES, VIRGINIA, THERE REALLY IS A HERMAN

But his life is stranger than fact—witness a last-resort gulp of flower water to extinguish a spicy food fire, a 24-hour rabbit watch and masquerade to save his vegetable garden, even an offer of someone else's baggage when the airline loses his... and, of course, more...! Syndicated in more than 300 papers nationwide, HERMAN skewers life with a stab at the ridiculous....

"IT'S CALLED 'MIDNIGHT SURRENDER,' HERMAN"

HERMAN

"IT'S CALLED 'MIDNIGHT SURRENDER,' HERMAN"

BY
JIM UNGER

A SIGNET BOOK

NEW AMERICAN LIBRARY

PUBLISHED BY
THE NEW AMERICAN LIBRARY
OF CANADA LIMITED

Published by arrangement with Andrews, McMeel & Parker

The cartoons in *"IT'S CALLED 'MIDNIGHT
SURRENDER,' HERMAN"* all appeared originally in *The
Second Herman Treasury.*

"Herman" is syndicated internationally by Universal Press
Syndicate.

First Printing, September, 1986

2   3   4   5   6   7   8   9

SIGNET TRADEMARK REG. U.S. PAT. OFF. AND FOREIGN COUNTRIES
REGISTERED TRADEMARK — MARCA REGISTRADA
HECHO EN WINNIPEG, CANADA

SIGNET, SIGNET CLASSIC, MENTOR, ONYX, PLUME, MERIDIAN
AND NAL BOOKS are published in Canada by The New American
Library of Canada, Limited, 81 Mack Avenue, Scarborough,
Ontario, Canada M1L 1M8
PRINTED IN CANADA
COVER PRINTED IN U.S.A.

"The rabbits are eating all his carrots."

"You're not getting an encyclopedia! You can walk to school like I had to."

"Nice to meet you at last. You must be 'Linebacker.'"

"How much longer you gonna be in here? The bread ran out last week and now the coffee and butter are gone."

"Drop it!"

"I know you're a veterinarian. Regular
doctors won't touch him!"

"This fortune cookie says, 'Very sorry, your overcoat stolen.'"

"You can put your left down now."

"Give me about a week's warning before they let
you out of here and I'll give the kitchen the
old 'once-over.'"

"$84 for labor! Wow, what an honor! Johnny
Carson changed my plugs."

"Forget about me meeting the willowy blonde! I
just need the name of one horse."

"Watch this! It'll go in two bites."

"Boy, that takes me back! I haven't seen a suit like
that for 30 years."

"Is it too spicy?"

"Mother's sent you a book for your birthday.
She says, 'Tell him it's got lots of pictures.'"

"Hey, boss! This cute little fella wants to know why
we're three years behind with the car payment."

"Did you mean for it to go in the lake?"

"In describing your 'general physical appearance,' I'll just say you're looking for a girl with a good sense of humor."

"We've lost your stuff, but you get first choice
of any bag off Flight 601 from Athens."

"What do you mean, 'Where's the car?'
This is the car."

"Don't stand too close; you'll make them homesick!"

"Mr. Soames here is the best teacher we have."

"Dig up your father or you won't get any
ice cream."

"There are two bedrooms on this floor."

"What have you done to your hair?"

"No don't switch it on; just explain the advantages over other insect repellents."

"One day you'll realize that the people capable
of running the country are too smart to get
into politics."

"We've got the same grandchildren! Are you
my first husband Harold?"

"Your wife's got a very bad case of sunburn
on her tongue."

"Where d'yer keep the bubblegum?"

"You here again?"

"Hey Bill, Bill!"

"Take my advice: Get yourself a good strong
woman and don't worry about looks!"

"It says:
'Due to rising costs, all wishes are
now 50 cents.'"

"Don't you people ever feed these
animals?"

"They're all out, but I'll tell them you called."

"I'm not worried. If I'm not smart enough to get a good job, I can always teach."

"Never missed a beat!"

"In some parts of the world, whole villages
could live on your food intake."

"Can you see anything?"

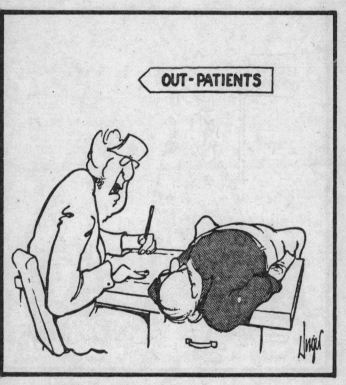

"Surely you must know if you have
health insurance..."

"Your father lost a dollar here in 1968."

"The computer is demanding a
complete service overhaul every six
months and two weeks off in August."

"Don't be a grouch. He's been waiting all day
for you to smoke that."

"Read it yourself! It says, 'Dozen eggs, bread, milk, chocolate chip cookies.'"

"Did you tell him 'Babylon' was a race-
horse who liked to run on the outside?"

"Don't ask questions. Just see if my umbrella's under the sink."

"She came straight out of 'Jams and Jellies'
without signaling."

"D'you mind showing me what you have in this pocket?"

"Don't tell me what it is until I've eaten it."

"I'll pay for them and we'll call it your
birthday present."

"You're a lot uglier than your pictures."

"If I find out you're faking, there'll be no 'yummies' for a week."

"I bet they try to keep our $5 deposit!"

"What would the 'widow's benefits' be, say,
six months from now?"

"Grandpa gave me his transistor radio."

"You here again, Carole!"

"We had a tough time getting that
stain out."

"Small, medium or large?
Or need I ask?"

"It's still raining."

"Don't tell me I'm getting HIM."

"What does the Guinness Book of Records say
about dishing out long sentences?"

"Dad put glue in her denture cleaner."

"It's hardly sex discrimination just
because I can't picture you as a topless waitress."

"A guy tipped me 20 bucks once!"

"It's my new invention. Talk to your mother for an hour on this and it will heat the whole house for a month!"

"We forgot the food!"

"Are you comfortable down there, Daddy?"

"It's your own fault for forgetting the can of cat food."

"Dr. Burns says you need two more appointments."

"What does he want to eat, a bowl of ants?"

"Watch out for that loose stair!"

"First time I've seen gold-plated tools."

"I told you not to wear
that dumb hat."

"Your shoes are marking the rug!"

"I get a real sharp pain when I do this."

"Snarl."

"You'd better not bring my brother anything!"

"Take a seat. It'll be about two days."

"I wouldn't call it a blind date. It was more like a
close encounter of the third kind."

"You're taking a chance, wearing
that dress in this neighborhood."

"The jury has found you not guilty, but I'm going to give you 2 years just to be on the safe side."

"You're absolutely right, I'm at the wrong house."

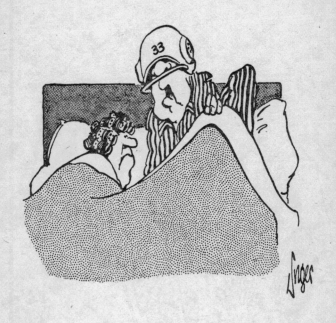

"I don't care what I look like, I'm not getting
mutilated by hair-rollers."

"That stove should be in a war museum."

"Your hat's full of cigarette butts again!"

"I'm sure you three will be pleased to hear I'm agreeing to your 15% pay demand. 5% each!"

"See, I got an 'A' in 'Disco Appreciation."

"At these prices, I've got about 20 seconds to recover and get out the main gate."

"You go and have your family reunion and I'll meet you by the penguins."

"He put our clock-radio in his sack!"

ABOUT THE AUTHOR

Jim Unger was born in London, England. After surviving the blitz bombings of World War II and two years in the British Army, followed by a short career as a London bobby and a driving instructor, he immigrated to Canada in 1968, where he became a newspaper graphic artist and editorial cartoonist. For three years running he won the Ontario Weekly Newspaper Association's "Cartoonist of the Year" award. In 1974 he began drawing HERMAN for the Universal Press Syndicate, with instant popularity. HERMAN is now enjoyed by 60 million daily and Sunday newspaper readers all around the world. His cartoon collections, THE HERMAN TREASURIES, became paperback bestsellers.

Jim Unger now lives in Nassau, Bahamas.